Jesus Therapy

*The Best Advice
Money Can't Buy*

By
Tom McQueen

Exulon
ELITE

Edited by Xulon Press

ISBN 9781498465632

www.xulonpress.com

Dedication

This book is dedicated to the men and women of East Lake Fire Rescue and their families. Our firefighters serve with commitment, competence, compassion, and courageousness in protecting our community. You have my deepest respect and admiration. I am humbled to serve as your Fire Commissioner.

Acknowledgments

I humbly acknowledge Jesus Christ as my Lord and Savior. I want to thank my grandson, Ethan McQueen, for being God's special gift to me as well as my very best friend. He wanted everyone to know that he is proud to be a student at Leila G. Davis Elementary School.

Preface

Look around—we live in a troubled world. The Golden Rule is tarnished and broken. The threat of terrorism cripples us emotionally. Corrupt politicians and business leaders nurture our cynicism. Our shock-and-awe media sensationalizes shootings, racial discord, sexual inappropriateness, and anything else that drives their ratings higher—all in the name of entertainment and exposing the truth.

Is the world that bad? Of course not, but the good that happens in our lives is seldom deemed newsworthy. Because of the psychologically proven principle that people move in the direction of their currently dominant thought, we are certainly stepping apprehensively, and despairingly, toward a very frightening future.

It's no surprise that mental health disorders are escalating in the United States, with record numbers of children and adults being treated for depression, anxiety, and panic attacks. For those who cannot afford a treatment option for what ails them, self-medication with alcohol, drugs, sex, and gambling, for example, only exacerbate their emotional pain.

Various media sources report that more than 260 million prescriptions for painkillers were written last year. That's roughly one for every adult in the United States. It isn't pretty; in fact, it's downright ugly.

Whatever happened to being created in the image and likeness of God? Haven't we been endowed with the three gifts of intellect, emotions, and will? With God's help, aren't we capable of managing the challenges and obstacles we face?

No one said life would be a cakewalk, but Jesus did tell us, "I am the way, the truth, and the life." When was the last time you heard that on the evening news?

We've lost our way because we have ignored our guide.

The Bible is the best mental health manual ever written. In this book, I'm going to share with you key lessons, particularly from the life of Jesus Christ, that will direct you toward a life of inner peace, contentment, fulfillment, and joy.

Table of Contents

God Made You: Be Responsible

He also said to the crowds, "When you see a cloud rising in the west you say immediately that it is going to rain—and so it does; and when you notice that the wind is blowing from the south you say that it is going to be hot—and so it is. You hypocrites! You know how to interpret the appearance of the earth and the sky; why do you not know how to interpret the present time?"
Luke 12:54–56

If there was ever a time in our nation's history when this scripture was applicable, it's now.

Undoubtedly, living in the United States of America are some of the brightest minds in the world. Our achievements in the fields of science, health care, and technology, for example, are indescribable in terms of dignifying the talents and gifts that God has given to each one of us.

Why, then, with all of the good that we have accomplished and the limitless potential to do even greater things, are we plagued by violence, war, hatred, racism, abortion, child neglect and abuse, as well as countless other crimes against humanity? The words of Jesus recorded so long ago are forever haunting us today: "Why do you not know how to interpret the present time?"

Actually, the answer is pretty fundamental. A nation that once placed God, country, and family first doesn't do so anymore. A nation that looked for ways to integrate gospel values with our nation's core values doesn't do that anymore. A nation that habitually raised its children to respect their faith, their family, and their flag doesn't uphold those values anymore. Thus when people make appointments to see counselors for help, their dysfunctional environment is simply a microcosm of what is transpiring in the world. We don't know how to interpret the present time.

As a marriage and family therapist who has treated hundreds of parents and children throughout the years, I appreciate, understand, and value the tools of behavioral science. Nevertheless, psychological theories and treatment methods are only as good as their origin and foundation. The only foundation that should matter to us as Christians is that our lives are born of God's love and His plan for each one of us. Being out of touch with that foundation and plan severely limits the success of any attempted counseling interventions.

As a counselor, I've read all the books, studied all the theories, and listened to all the lectures throughout the years. Most importantly, I've interacted with people who have come to me for help. Here's my conclusion: given the absence of any severe psychological disorder that renders a person helpless or incompetent, and understanding the legitimate need for medications when necessary, for the everyday problems and challenges that we Christians face, the best treatment plan is to, either on our own or with the help of others, invest our time and energy in reading, understanding, and applying the words of Jesus Christ to our lives, as He is the ultimate healer.

Counsel:

As you travel the pages of this book, make it something more than just a reading exercise. Have your Bible handy so that you can take one chapter at a time. Read not merely the quote at the beginning of each section, but the entire context of the passage. As I learned from all the people that I have counseled throughout the years, *Jesus Therapy* highlights the common challenges we all struggle to overcome. You may be experiencing one or more of them yourself. Use the words of Scripture, especially the words of Jesus as recorded by Matthew,

Mark, Luke, and John, to enlighten and enrich your journey back to heaven.

Prayer:

Father in heaven, help me to understand my purpose in this life and my role as a cocreator of the kingdom of heaven. In my secular world, diversions from Your way, Your truth, and Your life sometimes lead me to places I should never be. Forgive me for not waking up every day and thanking You for the incredible blessings that You have bestowed upon me. I want to focus on You, knowing that if I do, You will walk with me and always be at my side. Amen.

Your Life Is Important

Before you were born, I knew you. I called you by name.
                    Jeremiah 1:5

When we are moved to conduct demonstrations and marches today to make everyone aware that our *lives matter,* we are not paying attention to what God wants us to know.

We all matter. We were chosen by Him to come into this world. When you think about life, it's pretty phenomenal to realize that everyone we meet and interact with in the course of a day has been selected by our Father to be here. Just absorbing that simple understanding could alter the way we treat one another.

But here's the deal. We weren't just handed a ticket for the show. There is no such thing as being a passive participant in the performance of life. Because God chose us, we have a role to play.

When patients came to me for counseling over the years, sometimes they described life as a puzzle they couldn't figure out. My task was to help them discover that their piece of the puzzle was missing. Without their gifts, without their active participation in their families, work, and communities, the puzzle created neither a picture nor a presence.

There's a ton of reasons we can listen to about why we're not good enough. As a kid, I wasn't much of an athlete. When it came time for choosing sides, I was never the first player taken in a pickup game. It isn't like that with God. Everybody is a first-round draft pick. God believes that you are the total package.

It was Saint Francis of Assisi who said, "Lord, make me an instrument of Your peace." Having been called by name before we were born, is there a better reason for being in this world than to be an instrument of God's peace?

Counsel:

From this day forward, make it a practice to take ten minutes at the beginning of your day to sit quietly in a chair, close your eyes, and envision God putting His arm around you, placing you at this point in time, and reminding you that He will be with you throughout the course of your day. Talk to Him, and ask for His help. Make those ten minutes a habit. It will change your life. God gave us His only Son to die for our sins. Since He called you by name before you were born, can you give Him ten minutes to guide your day?

Prayer:

Father in heaven, thank You for the many gifts You have given to me. I haven't always used them in ways that bring You glory and honor. Often my hectic daily routine causes me to lose focus on what really matters. I'm distracted and sometimes detached from my real purpose in life—to know, love, and serve You.

Just as Saint Francis longed to be an instrument of Your peace, now I ask You to hear my plea as well. Today and every day, please fill me with the wisdom and the courage to be a hope and a help to my family, friends, coworkers, and anyone that I encounter on my journey back to You. Amen.

Anger Isn't That Bad

Jesus entered the temple area and drove out all those engaged in selling and buying there. He overturned the tables of the money changers and the seats of those who were selling doves.
Matthew 21:12

O h yes, Jesus was angry! As a matter of fact, according to Matthew, He was pretty livid. When you start flipping over tables in a temple, you're not exactly in your happy place.

Anger is neither good nor bad; it's just one of many emotions. What you do with your anger is the key to determining whether it will be a positive or negative experience for you.

If I listed all the triggers that precipitate justifiable anger in our world today, this would be a very long chapter. Suffice it to say that there are multiple opportunities to lose our cool on a regular basis.

The evening news reported recently that an elderly couple had their Christmas lights stolen when they went to church. As I listened to the reporter interview the husband and wife about the incident, I could feel myself getting angry. Apparently, the police officer that took the report of the crime was also outraged, but he chose to make it a positive experience for both him and the couple. On the day before Christmas, the officer delivered a Santa he had purchased for the couple to place on their lawn for the holidays. That gesture made a world of difference to the victims of a senseless crime.

Don't let anger's intensity paralyze you. It's unhealthy, accomplishes nothing, and can only deteriorate your emotional, physical, and spiritual well-being.

Counsel:

The next time you're as angry as Jesus was at the temple, take the two-question anger intervention quiz. The first question is this: is the issue important or unimportant? If the source of your anger is frivolous, then let it go by investing your emotional energy in someone or something that you care about. Seriously, is your world going to pieces because someone cut you off in traffic or called you on your cell phone by mistake?

Nevertheless, when your anger is justified, then move on to the second question: can you do something about it or not? If your anger is well founded but you can't do anything about it, don't let it permanently frustrate you. Give it to God and to those who have the power and resources to deal with it. However, if the origin of your anger is something that you can impact, then use your talents and gifts to make the situation better.

Prayer:

Father in heaven, sometimes I get so mad at the smallest frustrations in life. I make a mountain out of a molehill, and then I hold on to my anger so long that it ruins my day. Other times, I know that my anger is justified, but it still upsets me. Please help me manage my anger constructively. Give me the wisdom and the strength to understand anger as an emotion, then to use it appropriately and only when necessary in order to make a positive difference in whatever situation I find myself. Amen.

Emotions Are Normal

*When Jesus saw her weeping and the Jews who
had come with her also weeping, he became per-
turbed and deeply troubled, and said, "Where
have you laid him?" They said to him, "Sir, come
and see." And Jesus wept. So the Jews said,
"See how he loved him."*

John 11:33–36

W hen His friend Lazarus died, Jesus went
to comfort his sisters, Martha and Mary.
And when He arrived at the tomb where Lazarus
was laid to rest, He cried. In His human nature,
Jesus was no different than we are. He had emotions and He showed them.

Perhaps the greatest source of physical and
emotional distress is repressed emotions. I'm not

just talking about negative emotions; sheltering our positive feelings isn't healthy either.

When Cliff came to see me for counseling, he presented "anger issues" as his chief reason for wanting help. Initially, I asked him what happened when he got mad. He said, "I get so uptight on the inside that my face turns real red; then I clench my fists and I grunt."

Specifically, Cliff recalled a recent incident at work when a colleague made a comment about the results and quality of his assignment. Cliff came up with the usual red face, clenched fists, and a grunt, but he didn't communicate his frustration directly to his fellow employee. Eventually, Cliff found that expressing both his positive and negative emotions in a constructive way resulted in fewer red faces, clenched fists, and grunts and remarkably brought his blood pressure to a normal range while ending his long-time battle with ulcers.

One of the greatest discoveries that we can make as human beings is that our emotions are neither right nor wrong. Whether we laugh, cry, mourn, get upset, or jump for joy, it's okay. Having emotions is normal. Expressing those emotions and connecting them in a meaningful way with the events we encounter in life is the challenge.

Jesus was filled with emotion, and you are too. Don't hide your emotions. Share them. Manage them. Celebrate them.

Counsel:

No one can get into the habit of communicating their emotions coherently if they can't identify them in the first place. A great exercise is to be able to name at least one positive and one challenging emotion each day and then communicate that information to someone you trust. For example, "When I'm able to spend time with my children,

I feel _____," or "When I'm under pressure with deadlines at work, I feel _____."

Identifying and sharing at least two feelings a day will gradually cause you to be more comfortable accepting and sharing your emotions on a regular basis. The end result will be a more enriching connection with everyone that we meet on the road of life.

Prayer:

Father in heaven, what I have learned from You is that emotions are an important part of our daily lives. They have the power to connect us in a positive way with our spouses, children, family, friends, and coworkers. I know full well that our emotions can also be harmful, causing pain and turmoil for each one of us. I need Your guidance every day, not only to understand my emotions, but also to use them in ways that uplift the lives of my brothers and sisters. Please protect my emotional well-being and heal those emotions within me that are detrimental to my closeness to You. Amen.

Perseverance Makes Us Strong

Consider it all joy, my brothers, whenever you encounter various trials, for you know that the testing of your faith produces perseverance. And let perseverance be perfect, so that you may be perfect and complete, lacking in nothing.
James 1:2–4

I picked up my seven-year-old grandson from the bus stop not long ago, and as he jumped into the car, he greeted me with, "You wouldn't believe what a difficult day this has been, Grandpa!" Get used to it, Ethan, for there are plenty more where that came from.

Because we live in an imperfect world, we are all faced with challenges and obstacles. Some of us are tested more than others. Occasionally, our roadblocks are temporary; however, some of them are more permanent and require that we alter our life routes.

My work with our foundation and LegacyNationUSA has brought me up close and personal with life's most difficult circumstances. As a chaplain in a children's cancer hospital, sitting with parents who were losing their sons and daughters wasn't easy. Today, watching other parents neglect and abandon their kids is also painful. There's no shortage of personal tragedy and global strife in the world.

As a therapist, when bad things happened to good people, the question most often posed to me in a counseling session was "Why is this happening to me?" In fact, no one will find an answer to that question in his or her lifetime. A much more important question to ask is "How can I persevere and overcome the challenges that are facing me?"

In times of great adversity, I remind myself that life isn't a circular road that keeps coming back to the same location. Life is linear, and our path's final destination will bring us to a place of unparalleled and unimaginable joy and happiness. The one thing we need to get there is a relentless faith in God and His wisdom.

Our Father in heaven doesn't wish evil or hardship upon any of His children. Our mission is to trust in His goodness and know His plan is for us to be with Him for all eternity. Now that doesn't mean we turn over everything to Him and wait for a miracle to solve our problems. No, we are cocreators of the kingdom of God, and our heritage implies that we do whatever it takes to help ourselves address our challenges and grow in the faith that God gave us at birth. Perseverance in the face of adversity strengthens our character as God's children.

Counsel:

Perseverance is a three-step cyclical process. The first step is to embrace the comfort of knowing that God will be with you through it all and will never abandon you. Though the outcome of whatever is demanding your perseverance may not be what you want it to be, rest assured that God's will is certain to manifest itself to you.

The second step is to continually move forward on a daily basis, using whatever resources you can summon (both internal and external) to achieve your goal. Remember, not only is perseverance required in time of trouble, but it is also routinely required to achieve your personal, spiritual, professional, family, and marital objectives. Accessing an internal resource might mean relying upon patience or courage, for example. External resources might include parents, teachers, spouses, best friends, counselors, or the clergy.

The third and final step is to parallel your perseverance with your search for God's will. When perseverance first seeks the will of God in any challenge or goal, the probability of a successful outcome is always much higher.

When athletes are questioned about their ability to achieve some remarkable accomplishment, we're accustomed to hearing things like "I just reached down deep inside and found a way to win." That's just another expression for perseverance.

Remember, perseverance is a *cyclical* process. We don't just persevere for one day or one time and then it's over. In life there are multiple goals and challenges. Make perseverance your constant companion.

Prayer:

Father in heaven, some days I just feel like giving up, not trying any more. Life seems to throw more at me than I can handle. If I'm taking care of one person's needs, I'm neglecting those of someone else. I feel that I should be able to handle everything, but realistically I know that I can't do it. Sometimes I forget that You are with me, willing to share my burdens and to pick me up if I fall. In fact, I'm certain that my challenges are no more difficult than, and most likely less than, what others are called to face in their lives. However, that doesn't make it any easier. Please stay with me, help me when I fail, and give me the strength and the courage to persevere when the going gets tough. Amen.

Do I Have to Forgive?

Then Peter approaching asked him, "Lord, if my brother sins against me, how often must I forgive him? As many as seven times?" Jesus answered, "I say to you, not seven times but seventy-seven times."
Matthew 18:21–22

D o you think the act of forgiveness was important to Jesus? There's no doubt about it—it was. But really, isn't seventy-seven times overdoing it a little?

When I was the executive director of a non-profit counseling center, a board member wanted to make it a for-profit venture. None of the other board members agreed with her. When she didn't get her way and left the board, she sued me for nine million dollars. It was a ludicrous act of vengeance, and the jury, the appeals court judges, and the supreme court of Florida did not agree with her—not one person. But she had a lot of money and seemed to enjoy making my life miserable.

Did I feel like forgiving this person? Absolutely not! Did I forgive her? Absolutely. To be honest, my willingness to forgive wasn't forthcoming that quickly. I was pretty angry that someone I had trusted to engage in a ministry to benefit the disadvantaged now wanted to make money on the idea. In addition, I felt used and betrayed, and those two outcomes seldom engender warm, fuzzy forgiveness feelings.

In the middle of the lawsuit circus, I talked to God a lot. In prayer, the wisdom that He shared with me was to view the journey to justice as a learning experience. I knew that before I would be able to forgive, I had to let go of the anger that upset me. Gradually over time, with the help of my family and friends, I was able to renounce the ill will that imprisoned a part of me and slowly begin a process of forgiveness. Did I forgive seventy-seven times? No, but I did the best that I could, and Jesus never said forgiveness would be easy.

People sometimes say to me, "I can never forget what he/she did to me." Don't worry about it. Forgetting the wrongdoings we experience isn't necessary. It's the forgiveness part that Jesus made the requirement.

Counsel:

Are there people in your life, present or past, whom you just haven't been able or willing to forgive? Here's a thought that might help: The faulty assumption that people cling to when they are hurt or offended is that the perpetrator acted in a logical and thoughtful manner. That's seldom the case. Very often the people who do us wrong are acting emotionally, immaturely, and irresponsibly.

Remember, everyone is created in the image and likeness of God. The *person* that God created is fundamentally good. The reality is that the *behavior* of the person isn't always consistent with his or her character as a child of God. Therefore, when people act maliciously toward us, it's usually nothing more than a sophomoric attempt to *play God* and mete out some punishment they think we deserve.

Does that realization mitigate the damage and emotional pain that we might encounter? Certainly not. But it might just make it a little easier to forgive the behavior while realizing that the offender is still our brother or sister in Christ.

Prayer:

Father in heaven, forgiving others isn't my greatest strength. As a matter of fact, honestly, it's not a strength of mine at all. It's difficult not to harbor resentment and anger when I think that someone has deliberately tried to hurt me, especially when the pain doesn't seem to want to go away.

Please give me some small share of Your wisdom so that when someone makes my life miserable, I can rise above it and accept the fact that it's not about me, but about him or her. Pour Your grace into my heart and soul so that I might have the courage to say "I forgive you" and then continue my journey back to You. Amen.

Who Made You the Judge?

Stop judging, that you may not be judged. For as you judge, so will you be judged, and the measure with which you measure will be measured out to you. Why do you notice the splinter in your brother's eye, but do not perceive the wooden beam in your own eye? You hypocrite. Remove the wooden beam from your own eye first; then you will see clearly to remove the splinter from your brother's eye.
                                    Matthew 7:1–5

One of the things that I love about Jesus is that He seldom pulled any punches. He called it the way He saw it. If you were disingenuous, then you were disingenuous, and Jesus had no problem letting you know.

Now, the forthrightness of Jesus might be a little much in our twenty-first- century world, but is it really? The volume of phoniness and political correctness in society is at an all-time high. Under the guise of not offending anyone, the end result is that we are short on honesty when it comes to speaking our true thoughts and feelings. In effect, we become the hypocrites that Jesus was talking about, only on a broader scale.

What is also problematic is that we make judgments about others based more upon our personal biases and prejudices than on any factual information. Gossip becomes the communication medium of the weak, and the power of innuendo can tarnish the most honorable of characters.

Unless God made you His special earthly arbiter, it's probably a wise idea to stay out of the judgment business. Stay focused on knowing, loving, and serving Him, and God will take care of the rights and wrongs of the world He created.

Counsel:

Refraining from making judgments begs the question of standing against that which is obviously evil. When we know, for example, that the murdering of innocent people is wrong, we are of course called to express our critical opposition. What Jesus was talking about focused more on the personal attacks that one human being makes against another. Is it worth criticizing your friends and neighbors for where they go to church, the clubs they belong to, the clothes they wear, or the opinions they hold? Is that your purpose in life? Hardly.

If you find yourself in the mood to trash what someone is or isn't doing, give it a rest. You're wasting the time that you could be using to accomplish your personal mission in life and detracting from the energy that instead might be used to make the world a better place.

On the lighter side, enjoy this poem by Rod Hemphill. I'm sure you'll grasp the message:

HEAVEN

I was shocked, confused, bewildered
As I entered Heaven's door,
Not by the beauty of it all,
Nor the lights or its decor.

But it was the folks in Heaven
Who made me sputter and gasp—
The thieves, the liars, the sinners,
The alcoholics and the trash.

There stood the kid from seventh grade
Who swiped my lunch money twice.
Next to him was my old neighbor
Who never said anything nice.

Herb, who I always thought
Was rotting away in hell,
Was sitting pretty on cloud nine,
Looking incredibly well.

I nudged Jesus, "What's the deal?
I would love to hear Your take.
How'd all these sinners get up here?
God must've made a mistake.

"And why is everyone so quiet,
So somber—give me a clue."
"Hush, child," He said, "they're all in shock.
No one thought they'd be seeing you."

Prayer:

Father in heaven, as much as I despise people
who make judgments about me, I know that often
I find myself doing exactly the same thing. It's so
second nature that I'm not consciously aware until

later that passing judgment is exactly what I have done. Then I feel guilty and ashamed because I know it's not right.

So many people judged You during your earthly ministry, and each time You responded with such calm and compassion. I want to be more like You. Help me to understand and to accept the fact that judging people unfairly is not how I was created to behave as Your child. Open my mind and heart to accept the imperfections of others, realizing that no one on this earth today is without faults, but that all of us were created in Your image and likeness. Amen.

Accepting God's Kingdom as a Child

Amen, I say to you, whoever does not accept the kingdom of God like a child will not enter it.
Mark 10:15

Can the importance of our children be any more definitive than the words of Jesus as recorded by Mark in his gospel? I don't think so. Yet I haven't heard a homily or a sermon in the last thirty years that addressed the significance of what it actually means to receive the kingdom of God like a child.

In my work with children throughout the years, I've found three of their behavior traits that apply to what I believe Jesus seemed to have in mind.

First of all, children are like sponges when it comes to soaking up the sights and sounds of their new world. Having been most recently in the company of God, they absorb new information without filters. Adults, however, live in a world of "Yes, but . . ." and filter most of what they see and hear by applying their personal beliefs and perceptions. Thus the initial lesson that we learn from children relative to the kingdom of God is that we are called to accept it as they do, without hesitation or reservation.

Second, the natural curiosity of a child always wants to know more, understand more, and experience more. That's how God wants us to participate in the kingdom of heaven. He wants us to have an insatiable desire to make our vocation as a citizen of His kingdom a driving force in our everyday world. Be honest. How often do you think of your role as a citizen of God's kingdom?

Finally, young children wear their emotions like a badge of honor. Seldom do we have to ask them what they are feeling. In similar fashion, God wants us to connect with His kingdom emotionally and passionately. The kingdom of heaven isn't the Bible, a theological treatise, or a place we go when we die. God's kingdom is a way of life that begins with the passionate and enduring love that He has for us.

The lessons that children teach us are focused on accepting the kingdom of God without reservations and filters, enthusiastically embracing our vocation as citizens of that kingdom and realizing that we are its cocreators.

Counsel:

Children are God's greatest gifts. Two days before Christmas, I was partnering with a coworker in ringing the Salvation Army bell in front of a Publix supermarket in Safety Harbor, Florida. A little girl named Ava, maybe five years old, approached and placed twenty-four dollars in the kettle. Her parents said that she had colored about a hundred pictures and sold them for twenty-five cents each so that she could "help people who had nothing."

If you have children or grandchildren, the most important thing that you can do as a parent or grandparent is to invest your time with them and learn about what really matters in life. Kids have a special knack for keeping things real and not letting us get too caught up in the cares and concerns of our everyday lives. If you don't have children or grandchildren, there are plenty of opportunities to volunteer with meaningful children's groups and organizations.

Unless we focus our priorities on the children that have been entrusted to our care, our legacy as a Christian nation will be permanently and irreparably damaged.

Prayer:

Father in heaven, I can't get those words out of my head: "Whoever does not accept the kingdom of God like a child will not enter it." That's a pretty tall order in a world that seems to devalue the gifts that our children bring to us. I want to be able to clearly see the difference between *acting childish* and *living like a child*.

I need Your guidance and direction to replace the cynicism of adulthood with the wonderment of childhood. No longer do I just want to accept the inevitable; I want to see the possibilities for happiness and true joy through a child's eyes. Please bring back to life the child in me so that I can approach each day as dependent upon Your love and guidance as my Father, while risking everything to make the world a better place. Amen.

Cure for Depression and Anxiety

Come to me, all you who labor and are burdened, and I will give you rest.
Matthew 11:28

People get a little lazy in searching for cures to treat their anxiety and depression. See your doctor, get a pill, take your medicine, and you'll feel better. It's that simple. Really, it's not.

Let's make it clear that for people afflicted with legitimate mental health disorders, medication and therapy are definite blessings. The issue is that taking a pill or spending an hour in a therapist's chair is not the only tool of healing, especially when the source of the depression or anxiety is more situational than chronic.

It's easy today to self-medicate, and there are plenty of options: drugs, alcohol, food, shopping, sex, gambling, and a host of other options. None of them solve the depression or anxiety in the long term, and often they make it worse.

Other than maybe as a cursory prayer, God isn't usually the first choice—and often neither the second nor the third—for people to turn to when the going gets tough. The tangible cures offer immediate gratification, however shallow, even though the intangible help, God's grace, is much more powerful and effective..

A close examination of the life of Christ will reveal that He made Himself available to those who were hurting and in need of help. He will do the same thing for us; all we have to do is ask.

Counsel:

If you can imagine three concentric circles, the inner circle is our *real self*. This is where God wants us to live, using our intellect, emotions, and will to navigate the journey of our earthly travels with His guidance and support.

The middle circle is our *false self*. This is the dimension of our lives we find ourselves in when we drift away from what we know, believe, and commit to do and rely instead upon the opinions of others to tell us how they think we should live and behave. Unfortunately, when we become the followers rather than the leaders of our own destinies, conflicts often result that cause us to drift further from our real self to a very scary dimension of our existence.

The outer circle is the *medicated self* and that's where we end up when the misery of giving control of our lives to others becomes too painful of a place to exist. At that point, and often unwittingly, we medicate our emptiness with alcohol, drugs, and an assortment of other plastic pleasures.

Therefore, giving glory to the God who created us means making a concerted effort to live within our core, our real self, and employing the three gifts of intellect, emotions, and will to guide our daily journey. Will we make mistakes and travel forsaken roads occasionally? Certainly we will. But God understands that everlasting life is our ultimate destination, and He will give us the strength to get there.

Prayer:

Father in heaven, there is a lot of sadness, turmoil, and anxiety in the world, and occasionally in my life. When it happens to me, I feel disjointed and distracted. I lose sight of the important things, and most importantly, I feel lost and apart from You.

If I'm the source of my own worry, please help me see it, understand it, and use the gifts that You have so generously bestowed upon me to overcome and conquer it. I never want to be paralyzed by my inadequacies, but I always want to be enriched by Your grace. Amen.

Where You Place Your Time, You Place Your Life

When he saw the crowds, he went up to the mountain, and after he had sat down, his disciples came to him. He began to teach them, saying: "Blessed are the poor in spirit, for theirs is the kingdom of heaven. Blessed are they who mourn, for they will be comforted. Blessed are the meek, for they will inherit the land. Blessed are they who hunger and thirst for righteousness, for they will be satisfied. Blessed are the merciful, for they will be shown mercy. Blessed are the clean of heart, for they will see God. Blessed are the peacemakers, for they will be called children of God. Blessed are they who are persecuted for the sake of righteousness, for theirs is the kingdom of heaven. Blessed are you when they insult you and persecute you and utter every kind of evil against you because of me. Rejoice and be glad, for your reward will be great in heaven. Thus they persecuted the prophets who were before you.

Matthew 5:1–12

From my vantage point, this is one of the most important moments in the ministry of Jesus.

You can just imagine Him saying, "Let's take a walk up the mountain, find a comfortable place where we can sit down, and let Me share a few things with you."

The Beatitudes hold a special place in my faith because of the tremendous impact of what Jesus told His followers. All the while affirming that they were blessed, Jesus clarified the future for those who mourn, the meek, the merciful, the clean of heart, the peacemakers, the persecuted, and those who hunger and thirst for righteousness.

What is pretty amazing about the Beatitudes, when you examine them closely, is that they define most succinctly what it means to be a disciple of Christ. Moreover, what Jesus identified for His followers as being important is not beyond the capability of any man or woman created in His image and likeness. It is, however, a choice that we are called to make on a daily basis.

We are continuously assaulted with advice on what we should look like, what we should eat, what we should wear, and what we should do for a living, just to name a few things. Nevertheless, if all we do in our lives is to follow the words of Jesus in the Sermon on the Mount, we will most certainly be blessed with everlasting life.

Counsel:

With the frenetic pace of society today and the distractions that technology imposes upon our time and attention, how often do you think parents do what Jesus did with His followers? When do fathers and mothers say to their children, "Let's sit down in the kitchen or the family room for a little while and talk about a few things"? Moreover, how often do husbands and wives make the time to discuss the direction of their marriages and their families? Be honest. It doesn't happen as often as it should.

While the message of the Sermon on the Mount is one of the most powerful events in the public ministry of Jesus, the method by which it was delivered is equally as powerful. We need time to decompress from the pressures and stresses of our everyday responsibilities. Making time to sit down and with our husbands, wives, and children to refocus on what really matters in our lives is one of the greatest gifts we can give to those we love.

Prayer:

Father in heaven, what I would have given to be with You on that mountain when You shared the Beatitudes with Your followers! The guidance and the direction You gave on that day are exactly what we need in our time to heal the hearts and souls of a troubled nation.

In my haste to get things done, I spend too little time interacting with my family in a meaningful way. When I lay in bed at night, I feel sad because I have disappointed You and those who depend on me for help and support.

Just as You made the time to sit down with Your followers, please keep me aware of the value and the importance of investing time into the people closest to me. Let us use our time together both to celebrate the good things that You have given to us and identify the ways that we might be better partners, parents, and friends. Amen.

Life After Death

Jesus told her, "I am the resurrection and the life;
whoever believes in me, even if he dies, will live."
John 11:25

For many people, the subject of death is non-negotiable; they refuse to talk about it. For me, well, I died once, so I'm a little more inclined to be intrigued by the subject.

Death was my first life experience outside the womb, and not just for a few seconds. I was baptized and anointed by one of the nuns at the hospital. Something happened during those long moments before I was revived. I can't explain exactly what it was, but I've been taken back to that event many times during my life.

When people question the possibility of heaven, I have no doubts. When they are skeptical about what God has in store for us after our last breath, it's all clear to me. When people question why decent people die far too soon, I understand it's hard for them to discern the wisdom of God's time.

Heaven is a state of limitless joy and happiness in the presence of the Father who created us. When the world is no longer, heaven will always be. I believe that God in His wisdom understands everything about us. He even knows our unspoken needs and feelings. He gave us two great gifts: the opportunity to share in everlasting life and the means to get to heaven.

Heaven is what we can choose, and the invitation is permanent. Responding to God's grace is a choice. Our free will is the tool that enables us to decide whether heaven or hell is in our future. What Jesus told Martha is incredibly powerful—that He is the way, the truth, and the life, and if we believe in Him, we will never die. In other words, deciding to follow the example of Christ in this world is the path that leads us to heaven and enables us to celebrate forever with all those who have gone before us and with those who will follow after us.

Counsel:

Unfortunately, too many people think they have a right to go to heaven because of all the misery they have to put up with on earth. It doesn't work that way. Heaven is a privilege, not a right.

The vast majority of human beings invest their time and energy in the pursuit of earthly pleasures. There's certainly nothing wrong with pleasure; Christians, however, hold a different perspective concerning life's main mission. The understanding that they are on this earth for only a short time and that their sole purpose is to use their free wills to give glory and honor to God in this world so that they can enjoy eternity with Him in heaven shapes their focus.

Being a chaplain in a children's cancer hospital taught me more in one year than I've learned in my entire life. Talking to children and teenagers before they died, as well as to their parents, helped me to develop my beliefs about God's will for each one of His children. I was so touched by one teenager, Vickie, that I wrote the following article and published it in her memory. Follow her advice and your journey on this earth will lead you to your eternal home.

Vickie's Lesson

You'll never meet Vickie. She died on Valentine's Day. Seventeen years old is just too young to become a victim of brain cancer.

Vickie was the first child I met when I began my ministry at the Roswell Park Cancer Institute in Buffalo, New York. Stationed at a nearby parish, I was assigned to visit the hospital and bring comfort to the kids and their families during their illness and treatment. Truth be told, I always felt as though they gave me much more encouragement and support than I left with them—Vickie in particular.

She was fifteen when the headaches started. Her mom and dad told me she was the homecoming queen that year, a sophomore and the youngest queen in the school's history.

When I met Vickie during the Christmas holidays, she extended her hand to me and said, "Hi, I'm Vickie. The treatments aren't working, and I'll probably die soon. But don't feel sorry for me. I had a great life." I just stood there for a few seconds, searching for an adequate response to that type of honesty.

We visited and talked a lot in the two months before she went home to heaven. I remember one day asking her, "If there was a single, most important lesson that you learned in your life that would help me in mine, what would it be?"

After carefully considering my question, her penetrating blue eyes looked up at me and she said, "Well, since I've been here, I've learned that the Golden Rule begins with a verb." Not wanting to appear too dense, I asked Vickie to explain.

"Most people," she said, "wait for other people to be nice to them. They say, 'Well, if she's cool with me, then I'll be cool with her,' but the Golden Rule says, '*Do* unto others.' So the way I see it, we can't wait to see how other people treat us. We can make the world a better place by just doing it first."

Vickie went on to say that it was a lesson she had learned from the doctors, nurses, and patient-care staff at the hospital, who always took the initiative to make her feel like she was the most special person in the world.

I'm certain you'll understand why I couldn't share the lesson that Vickie taught me many years ago in front of a room full of people. It's just too emotional. But as you continue your life's journey,

I hope that you'll take to heart Vickie's words, "The Golden Rule begins with a verb."

Prayer:

Father in heaven, Your words to Thomas the apostle were so plain and direct: "I am the way, the truth, and the life." I need to go back to them often and remind myself that my purpose for being here is to follow Your way, accept Your truth, and lead a life that dignifies my role as Your child.

There are so many temptations in this world. Sometimes we are led to believe that today is the only day that matters. I know that isn't true, but refocusing on my vocation as a Christian isn't always easy. When I am in church listening to the gospel message, everything makes sense. Then when I am back to work or at an event, I sometimes slip back into my old shortsighted ways.

Please give me the wisdom and the understanding to discern Your will for me and the courage to live a Christ-centered life on my journey home to You. Amen.

What Is Your Gift?

You are the light of the world. A city on a mountain cannot be hidden. Nor do they light a lamp and put it under a bushel basket; it is set on a lampstand, where it gives light to all in the house. Just so, your light must shine before others, that they may see your good deeds and glorify your heavenly Father.
Matthew 5:14–16

When I was a kid, I remember seeing a photo of an impoverished-looking young girl carrying a sign that read: "God made me. God doesn't make junk." For some reason, I could never get that picture out of my head, and even today, I see it on Facebook once in a while. It's too bad that we don't all get the hint. God made us, and He doesn't make junk.

From the youngest of children to the most senior of citizens, I have listened to people who have no idea as to what their gifts are, let alone how to use them. Furthermore, when I reminded them that they were created in the image and likeness of God, a certain look of disbelief seemed to overwhelm them.

With all the classes and academic training that we receive in school, there isn't a whole lot of emphasis placed on coaching students to discover and employ their unique talents and gifts. Oh sure, we concentrate on sports, music, art, and a number of other worthwhile talents, but what about the gifts of empathy, understanding, and persistence, for example? Those intangible blessings can make a person's life incredibly powerful.

Actually, if our children have to wait for their teachers to help them discover their unique gifts and talents, what does that say about us as parents? There is no escaping the fact that mothers and fathers are the first teachers of their children.

It is incumbent upon them that from conception they talk to their children and, as their sons and daughters enter the world, help them to define, embrace, and employ their image and likeness of God.

Counsel:

If you can't see God's light shining within you, it is impossible to help anyone else see his or her light. That's just a small portion of the challenge facing our world today.

The first and most important task for all human beings is to understand that God has expressed His image and likeness within us. Once we have a clear handle on that, only then can we chart our own course in life and help others to do the same. Though talking to God in prayer about our vocation and purpose for being here should be our primary plan, seeking help and advice from others can clarify our future.

If our light must shine before others, we have to first see it within ourselves.

Prayer:

Father in heaven, I want to use the gifts that You have given me to bring You glory and honor. I know that my life is nothing without You. I spend too much time listening to what other people need and want me to do with my life. I know that they have good intentions, but what I really desire is to have the courage and the will to respond to Your direction and guidance.

When the clutter of the world is overbearing, please give me the strength and the wisdom to listen to You, not with my ears, but with the heart and soul You placed within me. That is where I want to find Your light. That is where I want to hear You speak to me. I love You. Amen.

The Case for Imperfection

Then Simon Peter, who had a sword, drew it, struck the high priest's slave, and cut off his right ear. The slave's name was Malchus.
John 18:10

When the disciples saw him walking on the sea they were terrified. "It is a ghost," they said, and they cried out in fear. At once Jesus spoke to them, "Take courage, it is I; do not be afraid. Peter said to him in reply, "Lord, if it is you, command me to come to you on the water." He said, "Come." Peter got out of the boat and began to walk on the water toward Jesus. But when he saw how strong the wind was, he became frightened and, beginning to sink, he cried out, "Lord, save me!" Immediately, Jesus stretched out his hand and caught him, and said to him, "O you of little faith, why did you doubt?"
Matthew 14:26–32

After arresting him they led him away and took him into the house of the high priest; Peter was following at a distance. They lit a fire in the middle of the courtyard and sat around it, and Peter sat down with them. When a maid saw him seated in the light, she looked intently at him and said, "This man too was with him." But he denied it saying, "Woman, I do not know him." A short while later someone else saw him and said, "You too are one of them"; but Peter answered, "My friend, I am not." About an hour later, still another insisted, "Assuredly, this man too was with him, for he also is a Galilean." But Peter said, "My friend, I do not know what you are talking about." Just as he was saying this, the cock crowed, and the Lord turned and looked at Peter, and Peter remembered the word of the Lord, how he had said to him, "Before the cock crows today, you will deny me three times." He went out and began to weep bitterly.

Luke 22:54–63

"And so I say to you, you are Peter, and upon this rock I will build my church, and the gates of the netherworld shall not prevail against it."

Matthew 16:18

Whoa, whoa, whoa! Let's hold on here for a second. Something doesn't make an awful lot of sense—or does it?

For a man who eventually became the first leader of Christ's church, Peter sure didn't have the greatest of résumés. If you were the owner of a company, would you want your CEO to use a lethal weapon on your behalf, have no faith in you when you were attempting to save him, and then deny three times that he ever knew you? Where is the wisdom in that type of leadership selection?

The fact of the matter is that Jesus knew exactly what He was doing. It's a huge lesson that we should learn from and employ in our personal and professional lives.

Peter was human and imperfect—impulsive, fearful, and emotional. He made mistakes—big ones, at that—yet after Jesus was crucified, died, and rose from the dead, Peter redeemed himself and led the development of the church in its early days.

In relating with Peter, Jesus didn't take a "do this or you're going to get fired" approach. No, He was patient and understanding, and He invested in those inner traits that made Peter a respectable leader in his own right. Jesus accepted imperfection and used it to fine-tune Peter's inner gifts.

Counsel:

Too often we look for the perfect spouse, the perfect friend, the perfect kids, the perfect job, the perfect boss, the perfect employee, or the perfect vacation and then are disappointed, sometimes bitterly, when perfection is nowhere to be found. Rather than demanding perfection from ourselves and from others, our expectations would be lifted and our anxieties relieved if we would accept the fact that only God is perfect.

Does that mean we give up trying to find peace and happiness in this world or refrain from trying to do our best in every venue of our lives? No, not at all. But we will experience a lot less frustration and fewer peaks and valleys if we accept the fact that ultimate perfection is found only in heaven. As difficult as life on earth may be at times, following in the footsteps of the perfect one—God—is the only vocation worth embracing.

Prayer:

Father in heaven, I'm too easily disappointed when things don't go my way. I want everything to be perfect all of the time. I'm so concentrated on the here and now that I seldom stop to see the big picture. I judge people for letting me down and not performing according to the expectations that I set for them. Rather than taking life as it comes, I try to engineer perfect outcomes in just about every aspect of my life. It makes me frustrated and upset.

Help me to let go of the belief that I live in my own perfect world because, as You know so well, I am far from perfect. Please give me the wisdom to understand Your will for me. By accepting the imperfections of others, I can also accept my own shortcomings. I pray that You will guide me along a path that will lead me to that one perfect place—life with You. Amen.

Genuine Faith Is Key

Jesus said to them, ". . . Whatever you ask for in prayer with faith, you will receive."
Matthew 21:22

Faith is the realization of what is hoped for and evidence of things not seen.
Hebrews 11:1

I have to admit that all those "do you believe?" mini team pep rallies before athletic contests appear to me to be more hype than anything else. Why would you have suited up if you didn't believe you could win?

I've heard a lot of disappointment throughout the years from people who have said, "I prayed so hard, but God didn't hear me and give me what I needed." Maybe they left out the part of the prayer equation that Matthew recorded in his gospel when Jesus said, "Whatever you ask for in prayer *with faith*, you will receive." Whenever I listen to someone say, "I don't pray as often as I should," it tells me that they might be lacking the "with faith" part even when they do pray.

Prayer is more than the recitation of words; prayer is a faith-based way of life. It is spiritual communion with God. If we believe in prayer as spiritual communion with Him, then our entire lives become expressions of thanksgiving, adoration, and supplication.

When we don't get what we think we need, and when it doesn't appear that God is hearing our prayers, exactly the opposite is true. God listens to our every word and gives us exactly what we need. Our challenge is to live each day grounded in the faith that He infused within us. That faith will enable us to accept and to successfully navigate even the most difficult of hardships.

Counsel:

Have I ever whined and complained when losing faith in someone? Yes. In retrospect, did it accomplish anything? No. It just gave me an opportunity to vent a little bit while driving a few people around me crazy. It's easy to lose faith in yourself, your family, your friends, and your coworkers. Jesus had faith in Judas, and look how that ended.

However many times it is tested, genuine faith is unshakable. The core foundation of every Christian's faith has to be placed in the Savior who suffered, died, and rose from the dead so that we might have eternal life.

If you haven't come to the conclusion that your faith in Jesus Christ is well placed, then the world won't make much sense to you, no matter how you look at it. The people closest to you can be experts at shattering your faith in human nature. Then, as you wallow in your misery while drifting aimlessly from your faith in God, life can quickly become a cycle of agony and despair.

Place 100 percent of your faith in God. He doesn't guarantee you an easy life, but He does promise life eternal to those who believe in Him.

Prayer:

Father in heaven, I don't want to be a doubting Thomas and have to place my fingers in Your wounds from the cross to know that You died for me. Life challenges my faith at every intersection. Too many times I neglect to recognize Your presence in my life, and I start to wonder if life is even worth living.

While human nature is frail and predisposed to temptation and weakness, let me never question my faith in You or what You have planned for those who believe in You. I know that Jesus said to the woman in the crowd, "Take heart, daughter, your faith has healed you." I place my faith in

You, my Lord and Savior. Please heal my heart and soul. Amen.

Compassion

When the Son of Man comes in his glory, and all the angels with him, he will sit upon his glorious throne, and all the nations assembled before him. And he will separate them one from another, as a shepherd separates the sheep from the goats. He will place the sheep on his right and the goats on his left. Then the king will say to those on his right, "Come, you who are blessed by my Father. Inherit the kingdom prepared for you from the foundation of the world. For I was hungry and you gave me food, I was thirsty and you gave me drink, a stranger and you welcomed me, naked and you clothed me, ill and you cared for me, in prison and you visited me." Then the righteous will answer him and say, "Lord, when did we see you hungry and feed you, or thirsty and give you drink? When did we see you a stranger and welcome you, or naked and clothe you? When did we see you ill or in prison, and visit you?" And the king will say to them in reply, "Amen, I say to you, whatever you did for one of these least brothers of mine, you did for me." Then he will say to those on his left, "Depart from me, you accursed, into the eternal fire prepared for

*the devil and his angels. For I was hungry and
you gave me no food, I was thirsty and you gave
me no drink, a stranger and you gave me no welcome, naked and you gave me no clothing, ill and
in prison and you did not care for me." Then they
will answer and say, "Lord, when did we see
you hungry or thirsty or a stranger or naked or
ill or in prison, and not minister to your needs?"
He will answer them, "Amen, I say to you, what
you did not do for one of these least ones, you
did not do for me." And these will go off to eternal
punishment, but the righteous to eternal life.*
Matthew 25:31–46

Jesus shared so much with His followers during His public ministry, but it struck me to know that He saved the allegory of the last judgment until the very end, just two days before He would be handed over to be crucified. To be sure, all the lessons that Jesus taught were important, but at the conclusion of His time on earth, it seemed that this particular story was as much a mandate as it was a message about our vocation to be a hope and a help to one another.

No one would argue that there is an abundance of self-absorbed, ego-driven people in our world.

Some of them proudly let you know that "it's all about me." That approach to living doesn't jive with being a servant to our fellow brothers and sisters.

The most common excuses people give for being reluctant to ease the burden of others are, "Where do you think I'm going to find the time to volunteer for anything, with my schedule?" or "I made my donation at the office. What more do I have to do?"

I can't speak for anyone whose main mission in life is self-gratification. I wasn't brought up that way. What I can say is that some of the most enriching and fulfilling moments in my own life occurred during times when I did my best to help others. And that isn't just my opinion.

At work we began a program known as Community Values Days. Each employee was encouraged and paid by our company to take one day a year to donate some time to a local nonprofit organization. They worked with groups like the Ronald McDonald House, Habitat for Humanity, the St. Petersburg Free Clinic, and the Homeless Empowerment Project.

Listening to the reactions of our associates after they completed a Community Values Day would have brought tears to anyone's eyes. Not only did it make them feel better about themselves, but the experience also afforded them an entirely new perspective on their vocations as human beings.

The allegory of the last judgment should serve as a blueprint for what each of us can do in our own way to make the world a better place.

Counsel:

Occasionally, when an individual made an appointment with me for counseling, I would hear a comment like, "I feel like I'm so alone, all by myself, and closed off from the world." In fact, that was often the case; however, in the overwhelming majority of circumstances, being closed off from the world was their doing and no one else's.

There was an ad on the television this morning focusing on Millennials and their expectations for a political candidate. In blurting out a series of personality descriptors, one young man noted that "we are self-absorbed," among other things. That doesn't bode well for his future and the likelihood of him experiencing loneliness, depression, and anxiety.

The legendary John Donne poem "No Man Is an Island" should have special meaning for us today:

No man is an island,
Entire of itself,
Every man is a piece of the continent,
A part of the main.
If a clod be washed away by the sea,
Europe is the less.
As well as if a promontory were.
As well as if a manor of thy friend's
Or of thine own were:
Any man's death diminishes me,

Because I am involved in mankind,
And therefore never send to know for
whom the bell tolls; It tolls for thee.

Counsel:

In the twenty-first century, do we really need to ask for whom the bell tolls? There are plenty of opportunities to embrace the allegory of the last judgment and recognize that the bell is tolling for us to engage and uplift our brothers and sisters, thereby giving meaning and purpose to our own lives.

Here's a suggested "compassion survey" based upon Matthew 25:31–46. Use it to measure your level of compassion.

A. Feed the hungry.

   1. Do I reach out to my family and friends when I sense that they are emotionally hungry for comfort and reassurance?

   2. Do I sensitize myself to the physical needs of the homeless, displaced, and abandoned?

   3. Do I support neighborhood and community projects that provide food for the hungry on a local, national, and global scale?

B. Provide drink for the thirsty.

   1. Do I make the time to quench the thirst of those who genuinely seek to know me on a more emotionally intimate level?

2. Do I express any appreciation or gratitude for those whose dedication and hard work make my life less complicated and more enjoyable?

3. Do I share the natural resources of the world by role-modeling good habits of conservation?

C. Welcome strangers.

1. Do I make the time to offer a pleasant greeting to strangers in the store, at the mall, or in my neighborhood?

2. Do I take the initiative to get to know new neighbors, employees at work, or the parents of my kids' friends?

3. Do I respond favorably when lost motorists ask for directions or when a person

in the grocery store asks where the baked goods are located?

D. Clothe the naked.

1. Do I pass my old clothing on to needy shelters, veterans' organizations, and other community agencies?

2. Do I respond to the pleas of the Red Cross for clothing when there has been a flood, fire, hurricane, or some other disaster?

3. Do I reach out and emotionally clothe those who suffer humiliation, embarrassment, and personal degradation?

E. Visit the sick.

1. Do I inquire about the needs of my family, relatives, friends, and coworkers when there has been an illness?

2. Do I visit my family, relatives, friends, and coworkers in the hospital for the purpose of offering my support and encouragement?

3. Do I respond to neighborhood efforts to prepare meals, run errands, or provide help around the house for someone who is recovering from an extended hospital stay?

F. Visit the imprisoned.

1. Do I make the time to share a message of hope with those who are imprisoned

by the walls of depression, despair, and hopelessness?

2. Do I inquire and respond in whatever way possible to the needs of those children, teens, and adults who are serving time in detention centers, jails, and prisons?

3. Do I sensitize myself to the needs of families and friends who may have a relative in prison and who are unable to provide for the basic necessities of life?

Prayer:

Father in heaven, I don't know how the world got to be this way. Some mornings I just don't feel like getting out of bed. All I want to do is watch television, surf the Internet, and avoid the hassles of dealing with obnoxious people.

Then, the more I think about it, I'm being nothing but selfish and stupid. I have responsibilities. I have a family. I rely upon other people and they rely upon me. Maybe if I focused more on enhancing the connection I have with others, I would be less prone to self-pity and isolation.

My prayer today is that You will grant me the courage and the strength to focus not as much on my independence as I do on my interdependence, and that You will help me to see that making an effort to touch the lives of families, friends, and strangers will complement the common goodness that makes us all one. Amen.

Is Marriage for Real?

He [Jesus] said in reply, "Have you not read that from the beginning the Creator 'made them male and female' and said, 'For this reason a man shall leave his father and mother and be joined to his wife, and the two shall become one flesh'? So they are no longer two, but one flesh. Therefore, what God has joined together, no human being must separate."
Matthew 19:4–7

J esus didn't say very much about marriage during His time on this earth, but what He did say was powerful. I was born and raised a Catholic. When I look at the programs offered by Catholicism to help create healthy marriages and renew hurting ones, it's phenomenal. So I ask myself, with all of the great counseling and services offered by churches of every faith to couples preparing for and presently in marriages, why do we see so many troubled marriages today?

Before answering that question, let me share some good news. According to statistics reported in the *New York Times,* about 70 percent of marriages that occurred in the 1990s made it to their fifteenth anniversary. That is up from approximately 65 percent of those that began in the 1970s and 1980s. Furthermore, couples who tied the knot in the 2000s are divorcing at even lower rates. If this trend continues, roughly two-thirds of all marriages will never end in divorce.

Nevertheless, if we get to the point where the marital casualty rate is one-third, that's still not healthy for our society. How can our faith help us to celebrate the love we have with our spouse while growing day by day until death do us part?

Counsel:

From my twenty-plus years as a licensed marriage and family therapist, I can say with conviction that there are two things couples must understand, accept, and do in order to have a strong, healthy, and happy marriage.

➤ Understand that "two become one flesh" doesn't mean that there is supposed to be a morphing of the intellects, emotions, and wills when two people get married. The challenge in living a successful married life is to learn how to complement the intellect, emotions, and will of your partner. Two people bring to the relationship the unique gifts that God has given them. Harmonizing those gifts creates a synergy that enriches them, their children, and every dimension of their lives.

➢ Accept the fact that married life isn't a static enterprise; you have to work at it. While marriage preparation programs offer some great principles to live by, as well as techniques to use in times of crisis, what really helps couples is a simple system that can guide their relationship throughout the course of their marriage. Intimacy is the foundation of a God-centered marriage, but it needs to be nurtured in six different ways:

1. Emotional intimacy: Being able to manage your emotions while understanding your spouse's and then openly communicating about them are key ingredients to strengthening emotional intimacy.

2. Sexual intimacy: It's important to understand your spouse's sexual wants, needs, and desires and to communicate about them openly in order to maintain a healthy sexual relationship.

3. Social intimacy: Your social network can be either a blessing or a curse in your marriage. Developing positive individual and couple friendships can enrich your marriage.

4. Intellectual intimacy: When husband and wife can openly discuss issues, ideas, and opinions without making value judgments about each other, they strengthen their perspectives on faith, life, and love.

5. Recreational intimacy: Having fun together is important in fostering a healthy marriage. Whether it's a movie night out, a morning jog together, or a game of miniature golf, discovering activities that are fun for both is an essential ingredient for a healthy marriage.

6. Spiritual intimacy: This is the most neglected yet most important element in every marriage. The couple who invites God into their

relationship on a daily basis through prayer is a couple who will always be richly blessed.

Now take a sheet of paper and score your marriage (individually and then together) on the six categories of intimacy, using a grading scale from A to F. Based upon the results of your survey, make and commit to a plan to improve your results.

Prayer:

Father in heaven, we spend so much time planning the reception, photos, and honeymoon that the spiritual significance of our wedding day is often lost amid the excitement. Little did we realize before we got married that after all the thank-you notes were sent to our guests, then the real work of a relationship would begin in earnest. Some days are good; some days are not so good. It's difficult when you're used to being on your own, and then all of a sudden, you find towels on the bathroom floor, or that last bit of ice cream you wanted is missing from the freezer.

It always seems to be the little things that send a marriage off track. Help me to stay focused. Help me to overlook the inconsequential matters that annoy me and to celebrate the joy of knowing that my partner said, "Yes, I love you, and I want to marry you."

Father in heaven, author of life, take Your rightful place in our relationship. I know that with Your light in our lives, we will overcome any obstacle on our journey home to You. Amen.

Loneliness Hurts

The report about Jesus spread all the more, and great crowds assembled to listen to him and be cured of their ailments. But he would withdraw to lonely places to pray.
Luke 5:15–16

My God, My God, why have you forsaken me?
Matthew 27:46

There were times when Jesus wanted to be alone, and then there were times when He was lonely. The same is true for most of us.

When I'm making myself crazy over people or situations, I get to a point that I need to take a walk, go for a run, hop on my bike, or just sit in a chair and be quiet for a little while. When that happens, I just want to be alone, refocus my energy, and center myself in God's presence.

There are other times, though, as I look back on my life, when I have felt genuine loneliness. I remember when I left school to work in a youth detention center. I lived in an apartment just outside of Albany, New York. I was ninety miles away from my family, for the first time living on my own. I had no money to speak of and no friends. For an entire year, I learned a lesson in loneliness.

Loneliness is an equal opportunity torturer. You can be a child, adolescent, adult, or senior citizen; it makes no difference. The pain of loneliness is pervasive and persistent. It takes a grip on your emotions as well as your thoughts.

In His human nature, Jesus knew that pain. The disciples who were His closest allies disappointed Him. Peter denied Him three times, Judas betrayed Him, and His disciples worried more about who was the greatest in the kingdom of heaven than they did about Him. When you feel that the people you have invested the most time with don't really embrace you, and a few even turn their backs on you, that can certainly precipitate a painful state of loneliness.

There are important lessons to learn from how Jesus used His time alone as well as how He managed His loneliness.

Counsel:

Interestingly, Jesus needed to recharge His batteries. In order to do that, He made the time to find a deserted place to go and pray. That's not often the case when the frustrations of the world get to us. We're more likely to react impulsively and say or do things that we ultimately regret. Our composure occasionally crumbles, and feelings of loneliness isolate us from our friends and family. Worse than that, rather than using a time apart to regroup our thoughts and feelings, we storm off and medicate ourselves with things that distance us from reality—food, shopping, gambling, television, alcohol.

When the world is getting you down, follow the example of Jesus. Take a few minutes, find somewhere quiet, talk to God, and ask for His help and direction. Listen to Him in prayer, and then return to what you were doing, refocused and refreshed.

If you experience a more pervasive loneliness, an isolation that is more than situational, one that would echo the words of Jesus in His dying moments: "My God, My God, Why have you forsaken me?" then patience and persistence need to be two of your most important resources. When Jesus was at that point of desperation in His earthly life, what we read in the New Testament is that He never gave up, He never quit, and He never regressed. With His Father's help, Jesus demonstrated a faith that caused Him to carry on and complete His mission in the face of doubt, scorn, adversity, and open hostility. In doing so, Jesus taught us that the strength of our wills is sufficient to lead us through periods of loneliness and emptiness.

Prayer:

Father in heaven, there have been times in my life when I felt so lonely, so helpless, and so abandoned. I'm ashamed of myself now for not placing my troubles in your hands. More importantly, I ask Your forgiveness for those times when I was younger and my prayers were more about what I needed from You than what I should be thankful for in my life.

When I take a closer look at Your life on earth, I can clearly see that You went through periods of loneliness far worse than I could ever imagine. I want to learn as much as I can from You so that I can handle those times in a manner that will bring You glory and honor. In my loneliest moments, I believe that You are with me. Thank You, Jesus. I love You. Amen.

Surviving Hypocrites

So the Pharisees and scribes questioned him, "Why do your disciples not follow the tradition of the elders, but instead eat a meal with unclean hands?" Jesus replied, "Well did Isaiah prophesy about you hypocrites, as it is written: 'This people honors me with their lips, but their hearts are far from me; in vain do they worship me, teaching as doctrines human precepts.' You disregard God's commandment but cling to human tradition."
Mark 7:5–8

Jesus had issues with hypocrites. Thankfully, He didn't have any reservations about letting them know. And guess what? Hypocrites have pro-created and multiplied, and they're still around in plentiful numbers.

Hypocrites are in every nook and cranny of our lives: family, acquaintances, coworkers, and neighbors. They're found in multiple areas: health care, politics, religion, and business. Some hypocrites ply their trade in sneaky, subtle ways and are very crafty, while the less sophisticated ones are easily recognizable.

Evil hypocrites are especially dangerous, as they have the potential to destroy people, relationships, families, friendships, and careers. With all their power, you would think that they would be pretty smart. In fact, the opposite is true. They're severely lacking in substance and morals, and they build their false sense of self-esteem upon the destruction of the lives of completely decent people.

Rather than just randomly using the term *hypocrite*, let's look at what the word really means. A composite of multiple definitions tells us that a hypocrite is a person who puts on a false appearance of virtue or religion while acting in contradiction to his or her stated beliefs and feelings. Jesus saw through the Pharisees and scribes and called out their self-righteousness.

I remember my grandfather giving me a sound piece of advice when he said, "Don't let your lips and your life preach two different messages."

Unfortunately, the father of three beautiful children never internalized that advice. His lips told his brothers and sisters that he was being a great dad, yet he didn't spend any time with his daughters and son, even on their birthdays.

The owner of a company didn't listen to Grandpa's advice either. He preached to the world that serving his employees was crucially important to the success of his business, all the while knowingly permitting a divisive CEO to put good people down at every turn.

And then there was the local politician whose pomp and circumstance would lead everyone to believe that he was all about supporting charitable community ventures during the holidays, when most people knew that he was lining his own pockets with the donations to a local Santa program.

Because we are imperfect human beings, hypocrites will always be with us. Learning how to manage them is the lesson Jesus taught us in His encounter with the Pharisees and the scribes.

Counsel:

If you've been fortunate not to have encountered more than a handful of hypocrites in your life and survived with little or no damage, consider yourself lucky. However, you need to be prepared. In reality, there are only two ways to deal with a hypocrite.

One way to manage a hypocrite is to ignore the phony. Don't get involved, and forget about confronting whatever lies or maliciousness the hypocrite is perpetrating. I've heard comments like, "Whatever they're saying or doing has nothing to do with me, so it's none of my business." That's the ostrich approach: stick your head in the ground and hope the evil goes away. I was never very good at that method.

The only other way is to follow the approach Jesus employed: confront the hypocrite. To be sure, that is seldom the easiest approach. As a matter of fact, it can be pretty difficult. Having said that, by choosing not to confront blatant hypocrisy, we give our silent assent to let it continue.

Hypocrites don't seem to know or care that nothing is hidden from God's eyes—neither their hypocrisy nor others' response to it.

Prayer:

Father in heaven, my character is full of flaws, and my life isn't always a testimony for doing the right thing. There are times when I've suggested to others what they might do, even though I've ignored my own advice. If I'm completely honest, hypocrisy has been a part of my life.

I need Your help to be true to the goodness that You have placed in me, and I need to make every effort, in every instance, to do the right thing. Keep me as far from the pitfalls of hypocrisy as possible, and nurture within my heart and soul some small sharing in Your honesty and integrity.

When I witness hypocrisy in the world, please give me the strength to address it in the same way that You constructively confronted the scribes and Pharisees. Please heal our world from the effects of hypocrisy, and keep us on an honest and straight-forward road to heaven. Amen.

What Gate Will You Choose?

Enter through the narrow gate; for the gate is wide and the road broad that leads to destruction, and those who enter it are many. How narrow the gate and constricted the road that leads to life. And those who find it are few.
Luke 7:13–14

Would you conclude that Jesus was telling His disciples that there are plenty of opportunities to do bad things in this world? It's a fact. Lying, cheating, stealing, deceit, and manipulation put a stranglehold on the values and behavior that Jesus shared with His followers.

The sad fact is that surprisingly few people seem to be very bothered by a culture wallowing in moral disgrace. We appear to have been anesthetized to what doing the right thing really means. Tell me honestly. How many times have you heard anyone genuinely ask, "I wonder what Jesus would do if He were faced with this decision?" No, we usually hear things like, "I don't care what you have to do to get the sale, just do it!" or "It's okay to bend a few rules; your job is to get it done." At one time, we could count on our parents, our pastors, and our teachers to be our guideposts. Sadly, that's not always the case today.

I would be lying if I said I wasn't worried about life after our earthly passing, especially considering the words of Jesus that those who find the narrow gate are few in number. What His words tell me is that doing the right thing is much more important than doing the easy thing. However, in today's world where "easy" always seems to be the preferred course of action, the road to heaven may be, recalling Robert Frost's wonderful poem, the road less traveled.

Counsel:

Sometimes it's a little overwhelming to know how much power we have relative to life after death. It's a power that God gave us when He formed us in His image and likeness with the gift of our free wills.

Choosing eternal life is a choice that we can make daily. Our behavior becomes the road map that lets us know whether we are advancing on the road to destruction or moving in the direction of that narrow gate Jesus mentioned.

As parents and adults, not only do we have to examine our lives for any course corrections that we might have to make, but we also need to recognize that our children have an especially difficult road to traverse. Our vocation is to stand by them, guide them, and assist them in the development of their free wills. While there are many nurturing environments where our children can grow in their faith and relationship with Jesus

Christ, there are also cesspools of moral degradation where naiveté and immaturity can lead to frightening consequences.

Stay on the road that leads to the narrow gate, and be sure that your children are walking by your side.

Prayer:

Father in heaven, *temptation* is a word that I don't hear much any more, yet it's hard to get through a day without encountering temptation in virtually every aspect of my life. Society is replete with opportunities to lie, cheat, steal, and engage in behavior that brings out the worst in us.

It's so easy to say, "Well, if it's good enough for them, it's good enough for me too." Then, after succumbing to whatever the temptation is, the guilt is overwhelming. It's like trading short-term pleasure for long-term pain, a bad deal by anyone's standards.

Please give me the awareness to recognize temptation, the courage to face it, and the grace to overcome it. Nothing matters more to me than my relationship with You, and I know that giving in to the temptation for evil only takes me away from Your grace and Your love. Amen.

Building a Solid Future

Everyone who listens to these words of mine and acts on them will be like a wise man who built his house on a rock. The rain fell, the floods came, and the winds blew and buffeted the house. But it did not collapse; it had been set solidly on rock. And everyone who listens to these words of mine but does not act on them will be like a fool who built his house on sand. The rain fell, the floods came, and the winds blew and buffeted the house. And it collapsed and was completely ruined.

Matthew 7:24–27

The pictures that Jesus painted for His followers about life's challenges were always so vivid and clear. In this parable from Matthew's gospel, He summarized a concise choice for those who had been listening to Him throughout His public ministry.

Jesus wanted His disciples to know that just *hearing* His words wasn't enough. *Acting* upon them was the key to salvation. When I was younger, I remember my father telling me that talk is cheap. Our actions shape our character and reflect our beliefs and what really matters to us.

In all our lives, the rains fall, the floods come, the winds blow, and our lives are buffeted at every corner. In truth, there is no remedy that will help us endure these human trials and suffering. The only helpful choice is to *act* on the words of Jesus. Let me be the first to say that taking action is seldom easy. In fact, most of the time, it's absolutely terrifying.

Acting on the words of Jesus, though, doesn't imply that we are perfect in every instance. What it does mean is that we always do our best to understand and to follow His teachings. For the effort that we put into acting on the words of Jesus, our lives become less cluttered, less confusing, and more focused.

Counsel:

I did some consulting work for a company in Florida and spent a great deal of time listening to what the employees had to say about their CEO. The general feedback was that he was a knowledgeable and fair man, possessing great wisdom. Nevertheless, his message didn't seem to change very much over time, and that resulted in the rank and file becoming more self-directed, thereby focusing more on their personal goals rather than on company objectives. As a result of this disturbing trend, less and less attention was being paid to key business objectives, and performance and profit were suffering.

Our faith suffers and inevitably we suffer when we tune out the words and wisdom of our leader, Jesus Christ. Although we may grow up learning the principles of our faith and listening to Sunday sermons, that isn't enough motivation to *act* on His words and teachings.

To be sure, we live in an era when the demands on our time are enormous. Nonetheless, when someone tells me that they can't devote ten minutes a day to reading and meditating on Jesus' words in Scripture, they might as well tell me, "I don't have time for God." Keeping a daily focus on the words of Jesus in Scripture is something each one of us needs to do in order to keep our house on solid rock.

Prayer:

Father in heaven, I don't want to be on my deathbed, apologizing to You for the little time that I devoted to acting upon Your words. More than anything, I believe that You are the creator of everything that is good. When You said, "I am the way, the truth, and the life," I would like to think that there is no one who believes that more than I do.

My failing centers on the fact that I haven't kept a very consistent focus on Your life. I haven't made those precious words of Yours my daily food for thought and meditation. When I might have taken a few minutes to read a passage from Scripture, I was checking a hockey score instead. Too often my priorities have been misplaced.

I'm committing today to become a better listener. Not only do I want to hear Your words, but I also want to embrace them as my daily guide so that I can know You, love You, and serve You with the remainder of my days here on earth. Please help me along the road of life. I love You. Amen.

Is It Healthy to Be Humble?

Who among you is wise and understanding? Let him show his works by a good life in the humility that comes from wisdom. But if you have bitter jealousy and selfish ambition in your hearts, do not boast and be false to the truth. Wisdom of this kind does not come down from above but is earthly, unspiritual, demonic. For where jealousy and selfish ambition exist, there is disorder and every foul practice. But the wisdom from above is first of all pure, then peaceable, gentle, compliant, full of mercy and good fruits, without inconstancy and insincerity. And the fruit of righteousness is sown in peace for those who cultivate peace.

James 3:13–18

This letter of James in the New Testament is a letter in only the most conventional sense. Other than the address, it's more like an exhortation and focuses almost exclusively on ethical conduct.

Ethics is a topic that receives too little attention in our world today. Yet, if we closely examine how Jesus conducted Himself during His three-year public ministry, we see that His humble, ethical nature was always apparent. He spoke to the fact that He came to do His Father's will and saw Himself as a servant of God as well as a servant of the people. When His healing power could have brought Him public accolades and adoration, He left to be with His small group of disciples. When others challenged Him and mocked Him, He responded calmly and with dignity.

At every juncture, the humility of Jesus was the foundation of His ethics. He always took the focus away from Himself and placed it directly on the issue. Maybe that is why James was so direct in his letter by saying that if we think we're wise and understanding, how about showing it with good works? How about standing up for what is right and not just going along to get along?

As ironic as it may sound, the people with the healthiest psychological profiles are the ones who are the meekest and humblest. Those with the weakest profiles are the most arrogant and narcissistic. An executive once suggested to me that humility isn't always easy. It is, if we accept the fact that we are totally dependent upon God for our lives and everything that we have in this world. In that dependence, we find emotional health and peace of mind.

Counsel:

I appreciate the fact that James didn't mince any words in his letter. The life of Jesus made such an impression on him that it was obvious by his powerful language that he understood the urgency of his Savior's message.

Calling out those harboring bitter jealousy and selfish ambition, the letter of James commands our attention today. We live in a materialistic and competitive world that urges us to focus on things rather than people and selfishness rather than service.

James was quite clear as to where our energy needs to be directed: "And the fruit of righteousness is sown in peace for those who cultivate peace." Jealousy and ambition are vertical in nature; if we want what others have and climb over them to get it, the assumption is that we'll eventually be happy and content. It doesn't work that way. That road customarily leads to arrogance and unethical behavior.

Peace, however, resides in the horizontal dimension of life. It's something that everyone wants, whether they realize it or not. To the extent that our purpose is to build lives, families, and communities of peace, we will fulfill what Jesus described in His Sermon on the Mount: "Blessed are the peacemakers, for they will be called children of God."

Prayer:

Father in heaven, help me to understand that humility isn't a weakness and that bitter jealousy and blind ambition are breeding grounds for unethical behavior. More than anything, I want to be what Francis of Assisi wanted to be—an instrument of Your peace.

In a world that values possessions, prizes, and places of honor, please grant me the wisdom to see that a life of humility and service to others is the road that will lead me back to You. Amen.

Love: What Role in My Life?

*So faith, hope, and love remain, these three; but
the greatest of these is love.*
1 Corinthians 13:13

I n writing to the Corinthians about the three
great gifts of faith, hope, and love, Paul asserted
that love was the greatest of the three. John, in
his first letter to the Christian community, was
quite clear in saying, "We have come to know and
to believe in the love God has for us. God is love,
and whoever remains in love remains in God and
God in him" (1 John 4:16).

Often we think of love in a temporal context. We
worry that no one really loves us. We talk about
falling in and out of love, and depression shackles

us when we reach the conclusion that we don't even love ourselves. We commoditize love in the media, mistakenly concluding that we can find love whenever we need it. Misconceptions about the essence of love are rampant in society and cause us to drift further and further from its true significance in our lives and relationships.

When Paul wrote that love was the greatest of the three gifts, his rationale was based upon its eternal, not its temporal, dimension. John also clarified the power of that gift when he simply stated that God is love. Therefore, if we embrace the fact that we are created in the image and likeness of God, then we have the essence of love in our lives.

If that's all there was to it, our days would be an ongoing love fest with God at the center of our lives. Going back to that free will we talked about in an earlier chapter, though, the decision to accept and to express the love that resides within our hearts and souls is strictly ours to make. God doesn't force us to love Him. Nevertheless, the angst of those whose emotional poverty is defined by an absence of love in their lives can be traced back to their decision not to accept Jesus as their Lord and Savior.

Counsel:

We have such a wonderful opportunity to spread the love that God gave us when He created us in His image and likeness. In order to do that, there are certain fundamental realities that we must understand and accept:

1. There is no such thing as finding love in ourselves or in another human being. God has already placed His love within each of us; our choice is either to accept it or to reject it.

2. When we acknowledge God's love within us and strive to live according to His Word, our capacity for managing life's interpersonal challenges increases a hundredfold.

3. Making a conscious effort to mirror the characteristics of God's love affords us a greater opportunity to receive love from others.

Everything recorded in Scripture relative to the essence of love is based upon God's love for His children and the living example of love that He gave us in His Son, Jesus Christ. When we open our minds and our hearts to this great gift, we will be blessed with loving relationships with our family and friends.

Finally, love is a risk. Jesus took that risk every day of His public ministry. For those who struggle with embracing the risk of loving someone, the following story is for you:

Once there was a powerful king who fell in love with a poor, humble, lowly maiden in his kingdom. He was so rich and powerful that he believed she would be forever grateful if he married her and made her the queen. It occurred to him, though, that there would always be something missing in their relationship. She would always admire him, thank him, and respect him, but she would never be truly able to love him because she would always remember her humble origins and her debt of gratitude. The inequality between them would be seemingly insurmountable.

The king decided that maybe there was another option. He could renounce his kingship, abandon his riches, become a commoner, and then offer the woman his love. In doing this, the king realized that he would be taking a big risk. He would be doing something that would be utter foolishness in the eyes of most people in his kingdom, and perhaps even in her eyes. He would lose his kingship, and she might reject him, especially if she were disappointed at not becoming the queen. Faced with this choice, the king decided to take the risk. He believed, he said, that it is better to risk everything in order to make love possible.

Are you willing to take the king's risk in order to make God's love possible in this world?

Prayer:

Father in heaven, if only I could stay focused on the true meaning of love. I often don't do a very good job of loving others; selfishness and righteousness are my greatest enemies. What Paul wrote to the Corinthians seems so simple in that love is patient, kind, and never fails. It isn't simple for me. I complicate it with excuses and rationalizations that make sense to no one except me.

I need Your help. I want to learn from Your life of love. Not only do I want to be a child worthy of Your love, but I want those closest to me to feel loved and appreciated as well. Help me to stay close to You by living a life of love. Amen.

Who Is My Family?

***

*And whoever does not provide for relatives and
especially family members has denied the faith
and is worse than an unbeliever.*
1 Timothy 5:8

A frustrated wife with four children sat in
my office many years ago and complained,
"My family drives me nuts." I get it. No matter
what type of family in which we find ourselves,
relationships can be exasperating.

Jesus grew up in a family, and in all probability, there were times when Mary and Joseph
shared the emotions that all parents experience
with their children. During His public ministry,
Jesus had a family of disciples who obviously
tested His patience on more than one occasion.

But as Paul wrote in his letter to the Ephesians, God decided from the beginning of time to adopt us into His own family by bringing us to Himself through Jesus Christ, and this gave Him great pleasure. As members of God's family, we have a responsibility to act according to the privilege that He has given to us, and "driving people nuts" isn't exactly what God had in mind.

Paul didn't sugarcoat anything when he wrote in his letter to Timothy that we are worse than unbelievers if we don't provide for our family members and relatives. The word *provide,* in a contemporary context, means something more than material support. Just as Jesus was a hope, a help, and a healer to anyone who needed Him, our role as a family member is to offer whatever assistance we can to nurture and strengthen our families physically, emotionally, and, most importantly, spiritually.

Counsel:

One of the key things we can do for our families is to understand the difference between a healthy and a painful family system:

PAINFUL FAMILY SYSTEM	HEALTHY FAMILY SYSTEM
Withdrawn	Open and free
Self-centered	Others-centered
Blaming	Healing
Demanding	Encouraging
Rigid/inflexible	Open-minded
Rationalizing	Focused on reality
Sarcastic	Civil
One-sided	Opinions encouraged

When you examine the characteristics of a painful family system, you won't find the behavior of Jesus as He related to His family of followers. On the other hand, when you observe the traits of a healthy family system, you will discover many of the tools that Jesus adopted to touch the lives of those around Him in a meaningful way.

Who is your family? Everyone. We are all God's children, and in whatever family dynamic we find ourselves, our vocation is to be a hope and a help to one another.

Prayer:

Father in heaven, being a part of a family isn't always fun. Whether it's a family at home, at work, or in the community, there are sometimes misunderstandings, hurt feelings, power struggles, and too many broken relationships.

Familiarity doesn't have to breed contempt. Relationships don't need to be about manipulation, judgment, and control. Life is so short, and each day that we spend not talking to a family member or treating them badly is a lost opportunity.

Our families, wherever they are, should be safe havens for husbands, wives, children, grandparents, relatives, and friends to grow and to live out their calling as Your sons and daughters in peace and harmony. Of course, there will always be disagreements and discord, but let us use them to learn more about ourselves so that we can become better people.

Please share with me the grace that I need to be a light of hope for my family, to uplift them, encourage them, and lead them to You. Amen.

When Hope Seems Hopeless

For in hope we are saved. Now hope that sees for itself is not hope. For who hopes for what one sees? But if we hope for what we do not see, we wait with endurance.
Romans 8:24–25

That's easy for Paul to say, that we should wait with endurance. But what do you do when your life seems so hopeless that waiting isn't an option and your endurance is depleted? That was a question that was often posed to me throughout the years by men and women who were attempting to overcome very painful life struggles.

In response to that question, I was always moved by what the Danish philosopher and theologian

Soren Kierkegaard had to say about hope: that it is passion for what is possible. There is a definite sense of personal responsibility inherent in that thinking.

Hope can never be a static state where we wait for something good to happen or for some knight in shining armor to ride in and solve all our problems. The odds of a successful outcome aren't very high in those situations. The passion Kierkegaard spoke about implies that there is energy on the part of the individual to keep moving forward, never giving up. The opposite of something static, passion is a dynamic force that seeks solutions, never content with stagnation.

Counsel:

The way most people think about hope is reflected in the statements we hear:

➤ I hope it's a nice day today.

➤ I hope I get the job.

➤ I hope my boyfriend likes me.

➤ I hope Mom feels better.

➤ I hope we can solve this problem.

➤ I hope I live a long life.

➤ I hope they have this color in stock.

The invocation of hope seems to fall into one of two categories: people hope for things over which they have no control, or they hope for things that they can control, but then do very little to influence circumstances to achieve the goal.

There's a no-fail plan for managing hope in our lives. When we hope for something that we can influence or control, it's important to passionately take whatever actions are necessary to influence the object of our hope. When we hope for something that we cannot influence or control, we need to turn that over to God, knowing that His plan will result in whatever is best for us.

Prayer:

Father in heaven, maybe it's a sign of my own weakness, but there have been so many times that I have felt both hopeless and helpless. As I look back on those times, I can see that many of them were of my own doing. When I hoped for something, it was more of an escape; personal responsibility wasn't a part of the equation.

I'm not going to hope that I do better. I'm passionate about following Your example and taking the initiative to influence what I can in a positive and constructive way. As long as I place all my trust in You, I know that my hope will never be hopeless. Please stay with me, guide me, and lead me along the right path. Amen.

Where Do I Go Tomorrow?

Come now, you who say, "Today or tomorrow we shall go into such and such a town, spend a year there doing business, and make a profit." You have no idea what your life will be like tomorrow. You are a puff of smoke that appears briefly and then disappears. Instead you should say, "If the Lord wills it, we shall live to do this or that."
James 4:13–15

For the better part of my life, I routinely asked myself questions like, "What am I going to do tomorrow?" "Where am I going tomorrow?" and "How am I going to get there?" It wasn't that I didn't know my next day's schedule or what my daily responsibilities entailed. It was more to the point that I needed to know how my daily activities fit into the overall plan that God had for me.

Life can get crazy. Clutter abounds. The burgeoning influence of social media, however positive in many respects, very often diverts our attention from the more important aspects of life and relationships to a plastic world of fantasy and frivolity.

As time passes, it's convenient to look back and remember all the times that "Someday I'll . . ." was the mantra that guided us. Then, all of a sudden, the reality becomes all too evident that there aren't many more "somedays" left.

James had it right when he wrote: "You have no idea what your life will be like tomorrow. You are a puff of smoke that appears briefly and then disappears." When I read that passage many years ago, I asked myself, if my puff of smoke were visible, what kind of image would it leave? I concluded that the image would be positive only if was shaped by following the words and actions of Jesus Christ, so I tried by best to plan my tomorrows with that goal in mind.

Counsel:

In a world where narcissism and self-aggrandizement are epidemic, there are more than a few who will summarily dismiss James's characterization that we are nothing more than a puff of smoke. Let's be clear that in no way was he dismissing our worth as children of God; rather, his emphasis was on the fact that we journey this earth for only a short time.

Having said that, a healthy approach to each day is to make whatever plans are necessary to manage life's daily responsibilities and commitments. The first step in the planning process, however, should be to ask God to guide our choices in a way that gives glory and honor to Him. In that way, our tomorrows will always be graced with His presence and love.

Prayer:

Father in heaven, I want You to be a part of all my tomorrows until I find my way to Your heavenly home. Please keep me focused on Your words and actions, and give me relief from the distractions that cause me to lose focus and momentum in my mission to serve You.

While secularism seems to permeate every dimension of my temporary travels on earth, help me always to see and to feel Your presence in my daily life. Direct my daily plans in a way that will cause me to see Your goodness in others and to serve my brothers and sisters in a helpful, meaningful way. Amen.

Epilogue

The choice to follow Jesus and act upon His words is reflected daily in the lives and actions of the young and the old. Too infrequently do we hear about those life-altering events that cause one human being to have a monumentally positive impact upon another human being. In our secular world, such occasions aren't deemed newsworthy, yet they occur in people's lives, families, and neighborhoods all over the world.

"Ethan's Presence" is a Christmas parable based upon a true story describing one of those life events. Sharing the story with you seemed to be a fitting way to end *Jesus Therapy*. As you read the parable, you will understand how beautifully and unmistakably Jesus intervenes in the lives of those who believe in Him.

Ethan's Presence

A Christmas Parable

O nce upon a time in a small, peaceful, southern village, a very busy family learned one of the most important lessons of life on Christmas Eve.

Oh, maybe fifty years ago, Madison wasn't the serene community that it is today. It was stunned one night when Chuck Miller, a young Vietnam veteran who had returned from combat duty only a few months earlier, was pulled over at Herthum Ridge for speeding and drunk driving. As the deputy sheriff was approaching the red Chevrolet, Chuck rolled down the window, shot the officer point-blank in the chest, and then turned the gun on himself and took his own life.

Nothing like that had ever happened in Madison before. The community was in shock. The deputy sheriff, Matt Thompson, was the mayor's son and one of Chuck's high school classmates. Matt's wife had just given birth to their first child, a beautiful baby boy, the week before the incident. Grief overcame the entire village as residents searched for answers that just weren't there.

About a year before he left for the war, Chuck had married Anna Redmund, the daughter of the general manager of Madison's only drugstore. Anna and Chuck had lived with her grandparents in a large two-story home on the corner of Highland Avenue and Lexington Street. There was no consoling Anna after the deaths of Chuck and Matt, but something disturbing happened in Madison in the following months.

Rumors surfaced that Anna may have had access to drugs from her dad's pharmacy and that she had been giving them to Chuck to help him cope with his experiences during his tours in Vietnam. As the wild speculation grew, it was Anna who bore the burden of blame for what had happened to the two young heroes on that sweltering August night. People said it was the combination of drugs and alcohol that precipitated the incident. Consequently, Anna was ostracized from the community and often ridiculed and harassed.

When she married, Anna was a young, successful commercial artist whose work was praised from coast to coast. As the months passed after the tragic shooting and the deaths of her husband and the deputy sheriff, she kept to herself, except when she went to the grocery store or to the local Catholic mission for Mass on Sunday.

When Anna's grandparents died some years later, she was left with their house on the corner and continued to work from home, seldom seen or heard in the community. Her neighbors often spoke ill of her at social gatherings and hoped that she'd get fed up and leave the village for good. Only then could they erase those sad and hurtful memories.

Anna, however, pursued her commercial art career in virtual seclusion and anonymity in Madison. She had no other family or friends in the village for the next half-century; that is, until she encountered a feisty little five-year-old boy named Ethan Thomas McAllister.

Ethan's family lived on the opposite corner from Anna Redmund Miller. Lifelong residents of Madison, Tom and Vickie McAllister were both high school teachers in the county school system and very involved with drama activities and coaching sports. They had not yet been born when Madison suffered through the Chuck Miller tragedy, but Tom and Vickie shared their parents' disgust over those horrific events and had never spoken a word to Anna for the more than ten years that they had lived across the street. In fact, they were so busy with school and coaching that they barely had enough time to talk with each other, let alone a neighbor they really didn't like or want to know.

Tom and Vickie were seldom home and often hired a babysitter to watch their son while they attended after-school activities. Little Ethan understood that crossing the street without permission or going anywhere near Anna's dark and dimly lit home was strictly off limits. But you know how kids are, especially ones like Ethan, with a little twinkle in their eyes and a devilish smile that tugs at your heartstrings.

Anna was seventy-five years old and retired. She'd often peek through her living room curtains and see Ethan riding his toy fire truck along the sidewalk in the summertime. Having never remarried and with no children of her own, she had often imagined throughout her life what it would be like to have a son or a daughter, but then the memories from her past would always become too painful, so she would return to her household chores for the day and to the relaxing artwork that she now embraced as a hobby.

It was a blustery day in October when Ethan boldly challenged the rules that his mom and dad had established for him. His kindergarten teacher had been giving the children a lesson on the importance of helping others and making the world a better place to live. Her words had made quite an impression upon Ethan, so much so that when his babysitter brought him home from school that day and he jumped out of her car, he saw that Anna's garbage can had been bullied by the wind and was now crushed against the McAllisters' mailbox near the street.

Just about the same time that Ethan got out of the automobile at his house, Anna had pulled into the driveway on her way home from the grocery store. He couldn't resist. He dropped his backpack, grabbed the empty plastic garbage can, looked both ways before crossing the street, and dragged it to Anna's feet in her front yard. With his sheepish grin and those sparkling blue eyes, Ethan looked up and said, "This is yours, ma'am. I think the wind almost blew it inside our mailbox."

As the babysitter screamed, "Hey! Get back over here now!" Anna stooped down to Ethan's eye level, smiled, shook his hand, and said, "Thank you, young man. That was so very kind of you. You made me very happy."

Of course, Ethan's babysitter had no choice but to inform Tom and Vickie of this egregious act, and summarily there was a punishment of no television for one week. It didn't matter, though. In his heart, Ethan remembered Anna's smile and how grateful she was to him for making the world a better place.

As time progressed and Anna got older, Ethan persisted in wanting to undertake his random acts of kindness to help her. Reluctantly Tom and Vickie gave in and let him perform what they joked was his "civic duty," while still keeping their distance from Anna.

A beautiful friendship blossomed over the years between the village outcast and the maturing youngster. Ethan would always look out for Anna, and as he grew, he never forgot to visit her for a few minutes after school or run an errand for her when she became ill. In return, Anna would bake Ethan's favorite dessert, chocolate chip cookies, and occasionally send them home with him to share with his family. On Christmas Eve, he'd always take her a special card with his yearly school picture, which she treasured and put on her refrigerator.

It was between Thanksgiving and Christmas one year when Anna died at the age of eighty-seven. Ethan was a junior in high school and was on a class trip with his hockey team when his parents called him with the news. He didn't say much when he returned home from his tournament. As he got out of his friend's car, he took a long look across the street at the old Miller residence, and tears came to his eyes. Then he carried his suitcase into his house and unpacked.

A couple of weeks later on Christmas Eve, the doorbell rang at the McAllisters' home. When Vickie answered the door, an attorney from the village was standing there, handed her an envelope, and then placed on the living room floor a huge, heavy, three-foot-by-five-foot package that he said was from Anna's estate. The envelope was simply addressed to "Mr. and Mrs. McAllister, the parents of Ethan Thomas McAllister." When Vickie and Tom sat down and opened the handwritten letter first, this is what they read:

Dear Mr. and Mrs. McAllister:

By the time you read this letter, I will have gone home to my God and to my husband. But I wanted to thank you before I left this world for the gift of your son, Ethan Thomas McAllister.

Not only has he always been a beautiful child with his blond hair, blue eyes, and never-ending smile, but he is one of our creator's truly precious gifts.

I never forgot the day twelve years ago when he returned to me my trash can that had drifted across our street. From that moment forward, Ethan's presence touched my life in a way that I never thought was possible after my Chuck died.

When no one else spoke to me about anything that mattered, Ethan did. When no one else cared to reach out and help a forgotten old lady, Ethan did. And when I became ill and worried about what would happen after I died, Ethan reminded me about what he had read in the Bible not long ago, that "whoever believes in Me will never die."

It would mean the world to me if you would give this gift to Ethan. It was over a decade in the making. I wanted Ethan to have it so that he will always remember what joy he brought to me. And please tell him how thankful I am for the gift of his presence in the latter years of my life.

God bless you,

Anna Redmund Miller

Just as they finished reading Anna's letter, Ethan hurried downstairs to find out what was happening. He saw his dad with his arm around his mom, tears silently streaming down both of their faces, and that massive package in the center of the floor.

"Is something wrong?" Ethan wondered.

"No," Tom said. "But I think that your mother and I made a very terrible mistake many years ago."

As Tom and Vickie explained who the visitor was that had just left, they pointed to the tightly wrapped package with the security seal and invited their son to open it. As Ethan carefully took scissors to the wrapping on the package, he discovered an incredibly beautiful painting of a young boy driving a toy fire truck in front of an old two-story house on a leaf-laden village street. The boy had a broad smile on his face as he looked toward the old house and saw the petite, gray-haired woman smiling at him and waving from the window. What set this painting apart and made it so unique, however, was the vague silhouette of an angel with a hand placed lovingly on the boy's shoulder from behind.

Ethan stopped for a few minutes, admired the painting, and smiled with a joy that his parents were seldom around to see. He ran his fingers across the center of the frame at the bottom where there was a gold plaque inscribed with these words: "Ethan's Presence." In the lower right-hand corner, the painting was signed, "A. Redmund Miller."

As Christmas morning dawned the next day in the McAllister house and Tom and Vickie were busy preparing dinner for the relatives and friends who would visit that day, Ethan sat up in his bed, looked out the window, and saw the home where Anna had watched him ride his toy fire truck when he was a child. Then, on the wall of his bedroom, perched high above the hockey equipment on the floor, her painting became the focal point of his holiday thoughts. Ethan Thomas McAllister felt at peace, knowing that in his heart he had already received the greatest Christmas present, just because he had wanted to make the world a better place.

About the Author

Tom McQueen is an award-winning author, executive coach, and founder of the nonprofit American Family Foundation, Inc. He has been honored as a recipient of the Angel Award presented by the Excellence in Media foundation for his best-selling book, *Letters to Ethan*. He has also earned two Indie Excellence book awards.

A sought-after speaker and workshop facilitator, Tom is represented by CMG Booking (www.cmgbooking.com). You can also contact Tom at LegacyNationUSA (www.legacynationusa.com), or you can e-mail him at letterstoethan@aol.com. Learn more about Tom's work as a corporate coach at www.tommcqueen.net.

CPSIA information can be obtained at www.ICGtesting.com
Printed in the USA
BVOW08s2008260816

460312BV00001B/1/P